THANK YOU FATHER, THANK YOU DAD

Story By
Yalonda E. Hampton

Illustrations By
Yulaine Poullain

YEAH Publishing House

CLR
Children Learn Resources

License Statement
This book is licensed for your personal enjoyment only.
If you would like to share this book with another person, please purchase
an additional copy for each reader. If you're reading this book and did not purchase it, or it
was not purchased for your use only, then please visit your favorite eBook or book retailer
to purchase your own copy. Thank you for respecting the hard work of this author.

YEAH Publishing House
Chicago, Illinois
Copyright © January 2020 by Yalonda E. Hampton
ALL RIGHTS RESERVED

No part of this publication may be reproduced or distributed in any form or by any means,
or stored in a database or retrieval system, without the prior written consent of
YEAH Publishing House, Yalonda E. Hampton including, but not limited to,
any network or other electronic storage or transmission or broadcast.

yalondaehampton@gmail.com
Scripture quotations are taken from the Holy Bible.
Digital and Printed in the United States

Dedication

A legacy of love, hope and relationship building, passed on from a dad to his son about his relationship with their heavenly Father. To our children, grandchildren, great grandchildren, and children afar off. It's your turn to believe and know that God the Father, Son and Holy Ghost is just one prayer away.

Listen my children to the instruction of your father,
and pay attention to him to get knowledge and support.
Proverbs 4:1

The prophet of God will turn the heart of the fathers to the children,
and the heart of the children to their fathers.
Malachi 4:6a

Hey dad, who are you talking to?

I was praying to God, Jonathan.

Who is God, dad?

God is the one who made the heavens and the earth
and that includes you and me and everybody son.

Where is God at dad?

God is everywhere, and his throne is in heaven.

Dad, where does God live?

His Spirit lives in our heart and in our mind.

Why can't I see him dad?

Well son, God is a spirit.
First you have to believe in him and then you will know him.

What is a spirit dad?

That is God's power Jonathan.

Can I talk to God?

Yes, you can Jonathan.

But I can't see him dad. How can God hear me if he's way up in heaven?

God can hear and see everything and
everybody because his Spirit is everywhere son.

God can see and hear everything and everybody dad?

Yes, he can son. God knows who you are and where you are.

Can I pray to God like you dad?

Yes, you can Jonathan.

Dad, what am I supposed to say to God?

You can thank God for making you who you are,
then you can thank him for making
your mommy and me and all of your family Jonathan.

Can I thank him for my new bike and helmet
and my reflectors and my vroom, vroom
on my tires and my space lamp?

Sure you can son.
God is very happy when we thank him for things that we have.

Dad, can you show me how to thank God,
so I will know how to tell him thank you every time?

Of course, I can, Jonathan.

How will God know it's me saying thank you?

God made you different from everybody else son,
and he can distinguish your voice from everyone else.
He knows who you are because God knows all about you.

Does God know my name dad?

He certainly does, and he knows what makes you happy and what makes you sad.
He understands everything about you Jonathan.
God even knows the things you think about and what's in your heart.

Daddy what's in my heart?

Let's see Jonathan.

Daddy, you're tickling me.

Do you love me Jonathan?

Yes daddy, you know I love you.

Do you love your mommy?

Daddy, why you ask me that?
You know I love mommy very, very, very, much.

Well, do you love your best friend Jordan?

Of course dad, he's my best friend.
We play rock monsters and ride our bikes together and
go on space explorations and adventures.

Listen to me Jonathan.
If you have love in your heart for God
then you will have love for others.

Oh, ok dad. Can me and God be best friends
just like Jordan is my best friend?

You surely can. God would like that very much Jonathan.
He will even be a better friend than Jordan.

Dad can we pray to God now.
I have a lot of things I need to talk to him about right now?
Can you show me how to talk to God right now? I want to pray to him.

Ok Jonathan I'll show you how to talk to God right away.
First, we have to be still and be quiet.
Then we have to humble ourselves Jonathan.

Dad, what does humble mean?

Humble is when we tell God how grateful we are that he loves us,
and we present ourselves to him and say here I am God,
I need you, I can't live without you and accept his right to lead and guide us.

Daddy do you need God?

Yes son, I need him very, very, much.

Why do you need God very, very, very much dad?

To tell you the truth Jonathan I don't want to live without him,
because he makes my life meaningful and joyful.

So, why don't you humble yourself then dad?

I do bow myself to God, to honor and worship him,
because I love and respect him.
Jonathan, when I humble myself to God,
I think of him first and then I can feel his power in me.

I want to humble myself too dad so I can feel his power in me too.

Ok son.

Should I bow to God and look up to him in heaven so I can feel his power?

Yes, Jonathan and God will show you how great and powerful he is.

But I don't know what he looks like dad because
I can't see him all the way up in heaven.
Can't he come down from heaven so I can see him?

What does heaven look like to you Jonathan?

Heaven is way up in the sky. When I look up in heaven, I wish I can go there and explore what's up there. It makes me feel like a superhero who can fly and turn into anything I want to. It's so big and it makes me feel powerful, but it's so far away that I have to put on my super invisible wings to get there, and see what God is doing up there.
Don't you want to see what heaven is like dad?

Sure son, I hope to one day.

Well, let's get in a spaceship and fly up there so we can see God in action.

You can't see God in a spaceship Jonathan.

How come? What about an airplane?

No son, not an airplane either.

Well, how am I going to be his friend and tell him stuff if I can't see him?

Come here son, let me try to explain to you who God is,
so that you can understand. God is a spirit.
He's like the breath that comes out of your mouth. You can feel your breath,
but you can't see it. Your breath is what connects you to God's Spirit.
God is supernatural and all powerful. His Spirit is everywhere all at the same time.
God's Spirit is Holy. You have to have God's Spirit to know him
and talk to him and feel his power.

I want to have God's Spirit, dad.
If I ask God for his Spirit will he give me his Spirit so I can feel him?

Yes, Jonathan God will fill you with his Holy Spirit
so you can know him and you can talk to him
and he will tell you the truth.

Dad, what is the truth?

The truth is what God says is right and it pleases him.

So, when are we going to talk to God so he can tell me the truth,
so I will know how to please him?
And so we can be best friends and do things together.

Honey, dinner will be ready soon, you can get ready for dinner too son.

Ok mom.

Ok sweetheart, thank you, we'll be there shortly.

Mommy, daddy's going to show me how to talk to God,
so I can have his Spirit so we can be best friends.

That's wonderful Jonathan. God is like the breath that comes out of your mouth
and he is the one that put his breath inside of you Jonathan.
God's breath is called Spirit. God is a Spirit that's why we can't see him.
We have to believe in him and his power son.

I know mommy, daddy told me already.

Ok Jonathan. God is like the air and the wind.
God is great and he is mighty in power.

I know mom, dad told me all about it already.

Ok, Jonathan when you finish talking to God
you can come to the dinner table and you
can thank him for the food that he has given us to eat.

Ok, mom that would be great!
I will tell God thank you for our food and for our family
and for our house and for everything else, ok.

Ok son, I would like that very much. I love you Jonathan.

I love you too mom.

Dad can we hurry up and talk to God now?

Ok son, come on let's go and talk to God.
Let's go where it is quiet so we can have some privacy.

Yea dad, we need some privacy. What is privacy?

Privacy is in secret or when you are alone
and close the door so no one will interrupt you Jonathan.

Close the door dad so we can have some privacy.
Hurry up dad we don't want anybody to interrupt our privacy,
so we can talk to God, so he can give me his-his-his what do you call him again, h, h, h.

Holy Spirit son.

Yea, so he can give me his Holy Spirit, so I can know him.

Now before we talk to God, we have to make sure we are not mad at anybody.

I'm not mad at anybody. Are you mad at anybody dad?

No son, I have forgiven everyone who did me wrong. After we forgive everybody then we can ask God to forgive us for the wrong we have done.

What if I don't want to forgive somebody?

You have to fix things right away son, so that it won't break you down.
Then you can have the peace you need to be happy.

Dad, what does forgive mean?

Has anybody ever did something wrong to you Jonathan?

Yes dad, Jordan broke my space lamp you bought for me.
I kept telling him to stop swinging it.

He did? You didn't tell me that.

Uhh....., I wanted to, but I was scared that you might be mad at me.

I didn't know that Jonathan. I'm sorry about that. Did he say he was sorry?

Yeah dad, he said he was sorry and that he didn't mean to do it. But I was so mad at first.

What did you say to him son?

I told him I was gonna tell on him! But he said he was really, really sorry.
So I told him that was ok. I'm not mad anymore and besides
you would buy me another one. Won't you dad?

Oh really, is that what you thought son?

Yes, dad. But it was not my fault.

I told him I wasn't mad at him anymore and we could still be friends.

Do you forgive me for not telling you dad?

You accepted his apology Jonathan because he really meant he was sorry,
so you let it go and did not let it destroy your friendship.
That's what it means to forgive.

Sure son, I know you meant well.
We'll try to always tell each other what is bothering us.

Ok dad, let's hurry up before it's time for dinner cause this is really, really important.

Let's get on our knees son and bow our head
and close our eyes so we can talk to God.
I want you to repeat after me.

Ok dad, I will repeat after you.

Heavenly Father.

Whose father are you talking about dad?

God is our Heavenly Father Jonathan because he made us just like him.
Well he made us in his image to be like him.

God is our Father, and he's our Holy Spirit, and he's my best friend.
Wow dad, that's one, two, three, that's three in one dad!

Yes son he is.

Dad, can I call my best friend Jesus?

Wow son! that's a great name to call him.
Now you will know who to call on when you want to pray.
We will pray to our Heavenly Father in the name of his Son Jesus.
The one who is your best friend.
I want you to listen very carefully to me, ok.
I want you to think about who you are talking to.

Ok dad, I will listen very good to you.

So let us pray. I want you to repeat after me Jonathan.

Ok dad, I will say what you say.

Ok, bow your head and close your eyes Jonathan.

Heavenly Father. Thank you for making me.

Thank you Father for loving me.

Thank you for everything you have given me, and everyone in my family.

Please forgive me for the wrong I have done.

Please help me to learn how to pray and obey you.

Please teach me to love others, and to honor and respect my father and mother.

Help me Father to follow the instructions of my parents and teachers.

I love you Father, and I need you, to keep your breath inside of me.

Teach me to love my neighbors and to forgive my enemies.

Please help me God to love you, with all of my heart, soul, mind, and strength.
Amen.

Heavenly Father. Thank you for making me.

Thank you Father for loving me.

Thank you for everything you have given me, and everyone in my family.

Please forgive me for the wrong I have done.

Please help me to learn how to pray and obey you.

Please teach me to love others, and to honor and respect my father and mother.

Help me Father to follow the instructions of my parents and teachers.

I love you Father, and I need you, to keep your breath inside of me.

Teach me to love my neighbors and to forgive my enemies.

Please help me God to love you, with all of my heart, soul, mind, and strength.
Amen.

Ok, Jonathan that was your first lesson in talking to God.
You have to talk to him over and
over again so you and God can know each other.

That wasn't very hard dad. I can do that, it's easy.
Wasn't it easy dad? Isn't it easy to talk to God?

Dinner's ready! Everybody come and eat so the food won't get cold.

Ok, sweetheart we'll be there shortly.
I think I heard mom call us for dinner son.
Anything you put your heart and mind to son is
not difficult if you believe you can do it,
especially with God's Spirit, he will give you the power.

I believe I can talk to God now dad,
because I believe he was listening to me.
I felt like he was there with me when I was talking to him.

I know Jonathan, he was with us when we were praying and he is with us now.
Now you can talk to him anytime you want to.

Thanks dad for teaching me who God is and
for showing me how to talk to our Father,
Holy Spirit and my best friend Jesus. I love you dad.

You're welcome son. It was my pleasure to lead you to our Heavenly Father,
and for our Heavenly Father to lead you to me, and I love you very, very much.

Until Next Time

Glossary

1. God- Creator, Maker of heaven and earth, Heavenly Father, Holy Ghost, Savior, Highest Being, eternal being, all powerful, all knowing, present everywhere, Living and True God

2. Holy Spirit- God who is spiritually active in the world. the presence of God as part of a person's religious and personal relationship for guidance and instruction

3. Jesus- Son of God, Savior of the world, the one who died for the wrongs of all people and rose from the dead and lives forever and is in heaven

4. prayer- talking to God with an honest heart in the name of Jesus Christ by the help of the Holy Spirit, giving thanks, confessing sins, praising God with adoration, calling on God on behalf of others, and humbly asking for something

5. spirit- the nonphysical part of a person, God's presence and power, the breath inside of human beings that gives us life that comes from God

6. believe- to place one's trust in what is binding and absolute, God's truth, accept God by his Word

7. truth- that which agrees with final authority and reality, the spoken and written word of God that is exact, never changes and is genuine

8. heaven- a place that is the home of God, angels, and of believer's after death, that is above the sky

9. power- the ability to lead or instruct one's behavior or the actions of others or the direction of events

10. exploration- the action of traveling in or through an unfamiliar area in order to learn about it

11. instruction- detailed information telling how something should be done, worked. or put together

12. love- show great interest and pleasure in someone or express actions and feelings of tenderness, compassion, adoration, devotion, respect, friendship, care, kindness, and desire

13. holy- dedicated or devoted to God for a religious purpose, sacred or set apart as blessed

14. forgive- stop feeling angry, stop blaming the person for a flaw, mistake or fault

15. enemy- one who hates another and wishes them injury, or attempts to hurt them, a person who is against someone or something

16. friend- a person whom one knows and has a bond of mutual affection, a relationship of loyalty and trust, those who keep an agreement with God

17. neighbor- anyone who comes into your life, is around you or a part of your surrounding for any reason and you show them love, compassion, kindness, and respect

18. important- of great value; likely to have a strong outcome on success, survival, or well-being

19. supernatural- a force beyond scientific understanding or the laws of nature

20. honor- have great respect and care for

21. apology- admission of wrong doing and asking for forgiveness

22. adventure- take a bold chance in the hopes of a good and positive outcome

23. humble- respectful, simple, not thinking of yourself to be more than you are, meek

24. grateful- thankful, glad, pleasing, showing pleasure for kindness

25. teach- show or explain to (someone) how to do something

26. respect- to cooperate with someone because you care about them and their relationship with you, to think about the feelings and rights of others

27. worship- making God the main focus on how you believe, act, behave, interact, talk, walk, pray, praise and devote your time and energy to him and do things God's way in your everyday life

28. soul- your character, personality, will, awareness, conscience, emotions, urges, mentality and strong feelings

THANK YOU FATHER, THANK YOU DAD WORD SEARCH PUZZLE

```
P I U Y T R E W O R S H I P H J K L X L
R E S P E C T P L M N K O I J N B H U Y
F T R D X Z S E W A D V E N T U R E L O
O R E S P I R I T I L O V E Y O U N T D
R H X W R A G B S N J T C V H F Y E J I
G M P A D B E L I E V E U A S A M I P L
I A L S I Y L K J H G F D E W Y P G C G
V X O T L N L R O I V S T H Q O S H R R
E B R O E A S L I A K W F R W S D B D A
E L A I N E Y T H U M B L E I P E O H T
J K T F V J E S U S C H R I S T R R T E
Y E I M P O R T A N T G O D Y U O Y U F
E N O X L A R U T A N R E P U S N E R U
H E N J O P T E A C H R E H K A O S T L
Y M S G H O L Y S P I R I T S M H F B E
B Y O X P L A I N F A I T H J O B R I A
L O R D F O T N O I T C U R T S N I B R
D S O U L G W M Z B L E S S E D A E L N
F A V O R Y I E E R G A C T S I N N E V
Y E S H U A P R A Y E R E P H E R D S O
```

WORDS TO FIND

- GOD
- PRAYER
- SPIRIT
- BELIEVE
- TRUTH
- HEAVEN
- RESPECT
- EXPLORATION
- FRIEND
- HUMBLE
- GRATEFUL
- HONOR
- SUPERNATURAL
- SOUL
- FORGIVE
- INSTRUCTION
- LOVE
- ENEMY
- NEIGHBOR
- ADVENTURE
- WORSHIP
- IMPORTANT
- JESUS
- HOLY SPIRIT
- APOLOGY
- POWER
- HOLY
- TEACH

Bible Scriptures

In the beginning <u>God</u> created the heaven and the earth. **Genesis 1:1**   *God*
So <u>God</u> created human beings, making them to be like himself. He created them male and female. **Genesis 1:27**   *God*

So anyone who refuses to obey this teaching is refusing to obey God, not man. And God is the one who gives you his <u>Holy Spirit</u>. **1 Thessalonians 4:8**   *Holy Spirit*
But when the <u>Holy Spirit</u> comes upon you, you will be filled with power, and you will be witnesses for me in Jerusalem, in all of Judea and Samaria, and to the ends of the earth." **Acts 1:8**   *Holy Spirit*

So <u>Jesus</u> was baptized. As soon as he came up out of the water, the sky opened, and he saw God's Spirit coming down on him like a dove. **Matthew 3:16**   *Jesus*
And a voice came from heaven: "You are my beloved Son; <u>Jesus</u>, with you I am well-pleased." **Mark 1:11**   *Jesus*

A man's pride shall bring him low: but honor will uphold the <u>humble</u> in spirit. Proverbs 29: 23 *Humble*
Do nothing from rivalry or conceit, but <u>humble</u> yourself and count others as important as yourselves. **Philippians 2:3** *Humble*

Jesus said: "<u>Love</u> the Lord your God with all your heart and with all your soul and with all your mind. This is the first and greatest commandment. **Matthew 22: 37-38**   *Love*
And the second is like it: 'You should <u>love</u> your neighbor as yourself.' **Matthew 22: 39** *Love*

But if you do not <u>forgive</u> others of their wrongs, your Father in heaven will not forgive your wrongs. **Matthew 6:15** *Forgive*
And forgive your people, who have done wrong things against you; <u>forgive</u> all the unrighteous things they have committed against you, and cause those who try to control them to show them humanity, equality and compassion. **1 Kings 8: 50** *Forgive*

The right time has come," Jesus said, "and the Kingdom of God is near! Turn away from your sins and <u>believe</u> the Good News!" **Mark 1:15**   *Believe*
Do not be worried and upset," Jesus told them. "<u>Believe</u> in God and <u>believe</u> also in me. **John 14:1**   *Believe*

And he said to them, when you <u>pray</u>, say, Our Father which is in heaven, Holy is your name. Your kingdom come. Your will be done, in heaven, and in earth. Give us day by day our daily bread. And forgive us our sins; for we must also forgive every one that owes us something. And lead us away from things that are wrong or unwise; but provide for us a way of escape from evil. **Luke 11: 2-4**   *Pray*
If my people, who are called by my name, will humble themselves and <u>pray</u> and seek my face and turn from their wicked ways, then I will hear from heaven, and I will forgive their sin and will heal their land.   **2 Chronicles 7:14**   *Pray*

THANK YOU FATHER, THANK YOU DAD

Story by
Yalonda E. Hampton

About the Author

Yalonda E. Hampton is a born again Christian. I am very family oriented with a passion to love and promote spirituality as an important part of spiritual health and well-being. My desire to share the good news with all people. It is because I have a personal and intimate relationship with the Lord and I have been in ministry with the Lord for more than forty years.

Being loved by God and receiving his saving grace through his Son Jesus is the best thing that has ever happened to me. Sharing my faith with others is a part of believing in God's Word and his power to regenerate my life, transform my mind, awaken me spiritually and revive my soul. Through this life changing experience I feel compelled to share this with others and especially to our youth who are most vulnerable to the world's attack of destructive devices.

You can connect with Yalonda E. Hampton via email: yalondaehampton@gmail.com and purchase **"Thank You Father, Thank You Dad"** and preorder a paperback copy.

www.ingramcontent.com/pod-product-compliance
Lightning Source LLC
Chambersburg PA
CBHW051259110526
44589CB00025B/2881